U.S. ENVIRONMENTAL PROTECTION AGENCY
OFFICE OF INSPECTOR GENERAL

Catalyst for Improving the Environment

Hotline Report

Region 6 Needs to Improve Oversight Practices

Report No. 10-P-0100

April 14, 2010

Report Contributors:

Christine El-Zoghbi
Eric Lewis
Larry Dare
John Coll
Ed Baldinger

Abbreviations

CANM	Citizen Action New Mexico
EPA	U.S. Environmental Protection Agency
FOIA	Freedom of Information Act
MWL	Mixed Waste Landfill
NMED	New Mexico Environment Department
OIG	Office of Inspector General
RCRA	Resource Conservation and Recovery Act

**U.S. Environmental Protection Agency
Office of Inspector General**

10-P-0100
April 14, 2010

At a Glance

Catalyst for Improving the Environment

Why We Did This Review

The Office of Inspector General received a hotline complaint from Citizen Action New Mexico (CANM) alleging that the New Mexico Environment Department (NMED) mismanaged the Sandia National Laboratory's Mixed Waste Landfill (MWL) monitoring wells. We sought to determine if the allegation had merit by reviewing U.S. Environmental Protection Agency (EPA) Region 6's oversight activities.

Background

The Resource Conservation and Recovery Act requires EPA Region 6 to provide oversight to delegated sites. EPA's Public Involvement Policy encourages EPA staff and managers to ensure that decision-making processes are open and accessible.

For further information, contact our Office of Congressional, Public Affairs and Management at (202) 566-2391.

To view the full report, click on the following link:
www.epa.gov/oig/reports/2010/ 20100414-10-P-0100.pdf

Region 6 Needs to Improve Oversight Practices

What We Found

Region 6's documentation of its oversight was not sufficient to determine whether CANM's allegations had merit or whether NMED's actions and decisions with regard to the MWL monitoring wells were technically sound. Specifically, Region 6 staff (1) took inappropriate steps to keep the details of the MWL monitoring wells assessment from the public, (2) decided not to provide documentation or sometimes not to document their concerns about the MWL monitoring wells, (3) provided a letter to CANM that did not note the specific details of the assessment, or (4) improperly placed a national security marking (Confidential) on the assessment. The Region's actions are a violation of EPA's Public Involvement Policy and EPA's Records Management Policy.

What We Recommend

We recommend that the Regional Administrator, Region 6, comply with EPA's national security, public involvement, and records management policies, including removing the national security marking from the December 2007 Oversight Review. As part of this recommendation, the Regional Administrator should ensure that the opinions of technical and nontechnical staff are documented to support EPA's oversight decisions, and develop or update oversight standard operating procedures to ensure compliance with these policies. We also recommend that the Regional Administrator evaluate the extent to which the Region has not recorded oversight information, or misclassified information, to determine the scope of administrative action or training necessary to remedy the situation.

Region 6 comments were not responsive. Region 6 disagreed with the report's conclusion and recommendations, stating that information was not withheld from the public. However, the Region also stated that the information was exempt from release under the Freedom of Information Act. Region 6 also denied violating national security, public involvement, and records management policies. Region 6 stated that marking documents "confidential" is a common practice "throughout the agency" for many (unclassified) documents. The recommendations are unresolved. Region 6 requested resolution be elevated in accordance with EPA's Audit Management Process.

UNITED STATES ENVIRONMENTAL PROTECTION AGENCY
WASHINGTON, D.C. 20460

April 14, 2010

MEMORANDUM

SUBJECT: Region 6 Needs to Improve Oversight Practices
Report No. 10-P-0100

FROM: Wade T. Najjum
Assistant Inspector
Office of Program Evaluation

TO: Robert Perciasepe
Deputy Administrator

The Office of Inspector General (OIG) of the U.S. Environmental Protection Agency (EPA) conducted this subject audit. This report contains findings that describe problems we identified and corrective actions we recommend. This report represents our opinion and does not necessarily represent the final EPA position. EPA managers will make final determinations on matters in this report in accordance with established audit resolution procedures. Region 6 did not agree with the conclusions and recommendations in the draft report and requested that the matter be elevated in accordance with EPA's Audit Management Process.

The estimated cost of this report – calculated by multiplying the project's staff days by the applicable daily full cost billing rates in effect at the time – is $272,846.

Action Required

As part of the audit resolution process, we are requesting you provide a written response to this report within 90 calendar days. You should include a corrective actions plan for agreed-upon actions, including milestone dates. We have no objections to the further release of this report to the public. This report will be available at http://www.epa.gov/oig.

If you or your staff have any questions regarding this report, please contact me at 202-566-0827 or najjum.wade@epa.gov, or Eric Lewis at 202-566-2664 or lewis.eric@epa.gov.

Table of Contents

Appendices

Purpose

In May 2007, the Office of Inspector General (OIG) of the U.S. Environmental Protection Agency (EPA) received allegations from Citizen Action New Mexico (CANM) alleging that the New Mexico Environment Department (NMED) mismanaged the Sandia National Laboratory's Mixed Waste Landfill (MWL) monitoring wells. We sought to determine if EPA Region 6 carried out its oversight responsibilities regarding Sandia National Laboratory's MWL monitoring wells.

Background

The Sandia MWL is a Solid Waste Management Unit site; the monitoring wells are managed by NMED. EPA Region 6 provides oversight to NMED according to a memorandum of agreement with the State of New Mexico. The site is a fenced, 2.6-acre compound that includes several monitoring wells and a background well.

In March 2007, CAMN requested that Region 6 review NMED decisions regarding the monitoring wells at Sandia MWL. The Project Engineer for Sandia stated that the Region became involved with the MWL monitoring wells only after the Region received a request from U.S. Senator Bingaman of New Mexico in April 2007. In response to the Senator's request, Region 6 replied that it was conducting an internal review of all well monitoring information, and that it would provide a response to CANM as soon as possible. Region 6 responded to the Senator and CANM in June and December 2007, respectively.

In December 2007, a team of three Region 6 technical staff and a project manager developed a detailed assessment of CANM's concerns. The team included two hydrologists and a geologist. The project manager was an engineer. The Region 6 team reviewed the overall MWL groundwater monitoring system in order to determine its efficacy in detecting contamination. The team reviewed well locations, depth of wells and well screens, purging and sampling methods, videos, and analytical results.

The Region 6 team's findings were summarized in a draft document titled "Sandia Mixed Waste Landfill Groundwater Monitoring Well System and Program Oversight Review" (Oversight Review). This document included comparisons of Region 6 findings and recommendations, NMED recommendations, and CANM issues of concern as stated in its letter of March 2007.

The EPA Public Involvement Policy, May 2003, supplements existing EPA regulations that prescribe specific public participation requirements. The policy applies to all EPA programs and activities. One of EPA's goals for this policy is to ensure that the public has timely, accessible, and accurate information about EPA programs. According to the policy, under the overall direction of the Administrator, Regional Administrators are responsible for ensuring that their managers and staff encourage and facilitate public involvement in programs and activities.

The EPA Records Management Policy, June 2009, established requirements for managing EPA's records. The policy promotes access to information by EPA staff, EPA partners, and the public, as appropriate.

The EPA National Security Information Handbook, December 2006, sets forth the official policies, standards, and procedures for EPA employees and nonfederal personnel who have access to classified national security information. Based on Executive Order 12958, the authority to classify original information at the Secret or Confidential level may be exercised only by the Administrator, EPA, and officials to whom such authority has been directly delegated by the Administrator, in writing. Information may not be classified unless its disclosure could reasonably be expected to cause damage to national security.

OMB Circular A-123, Management's Responsibility for Internal Control, December 21, 2004, states that management is responsible for establishing and maintaining internal control to achieve the objectives of effective and efficient operations, reliable financial reporting, and compliance with applicable laws and regulations. Management shall consistently apply the internal control standards to meet each of the internal control objectives and to assess internal control effectiveness. Internal control standards include control activities. Control activities include policies, procedures, and mechanisms in place to help ensure that agency objectives are met. These procedures include appropriate documentation and access to that documentation. The absence of effective control activities could lead to internal control deficiencies.

Scope and Methodology

We conducted field work from December 2008 to September 2009 in accordance with generally accepted government auditing standards. Those standards require that based on our objectives, we plan and perform the audit to obtain sufficient and appropriate evidence to provide a reasonable basis for our findings and conclusions. We reviewed documents, regulations, the New Mexico/EPA memorandum of agreement governing NMED's Resource Conservation and Recovery Act (RCRA) program, and annual and semiannual reviews. We interviewed EPA Region 6 RCRA program managers and technical experts who work with New Mexico. We also interviewed members of CANM.

We believe that the evidence obtained provides a reasonable basis for our findings and conclusions based on our audit objectives. EPA has granted the State of New Mexico primary responsibility for enforcing the RCRA program within its boundaries. We limited our review to EPA's oversight responsibilities as defined in applicable regulations and the memorandum of agreement with the State

Results of Review: Lack of Transparency Obscures Assessing Whether NMED Was Effectively Managing the MWL Monitoring Wells

Region 6's lack of documentation of its oversight prevented the OIG from determining whether CANM's allegations had merit. The Region's lack of documentation also prevented the OIG from assessing whether NMED's actions and decisions with regard to the MWL monitoring wells were technically sound. Specifically, the Region did not provide the OIG with documentation to support the Region 6 response to CANM that the Region found NMED's overall actions and decisions to be technically sound and consistent with requirements. We found that some Region 6 staff members intentionally did not document their oversight of the

Sandia MWL monitoring wells. The Chief of the Federal Facilities Section and Project Engineer for Sandia also limited public involvement by withholding information regarding the MWL monitoring wells and dismissing the Region's concerns about the site without documenting their decisions.

Region 6 Actions Limit Public Involvement

Region 6 withheld information from the public regarding the MWL monitoring wells through:

- discontinuation of record keeping,
- misleading communications, and
- inappropriate classification.

Discontinuation of Record Keeping. The Region 6 Project Engineer for Sandia stated that her section discontinued record keeping in favor of undocumented phone calls and conversations with NMED to prevent the production of documents. During an interview with the OIG, the Project Engineer for Sandia informed us that her section had discontinued record keeping of phone calls and discussions between the Region and NMED because of CANM's requests for documentation regarding the MWL, including extensive requests for information under the Freedom of Information Act. According to EPA's Records Management Policy, the Federal Records Act of 1950, as amended, requires all federal agencies to make and preserve records containing adequate and proper documentation of their organization, function, policies, decisions, procedures, and essential transactions. The policy requires EPA offices to create, receive, and maintain official records providing adequate and proper documentation and evidence of EPA's activities.

The Region 6 Chief of the Federal Facilities Section further noted that NMED "has become reluctant to engage in open discussions with Region 6 in order to avoid CA[NM]'s distortion of facts, repetitive Freedom of Information Act (FOIA) requests, and threats of lawsuits." Consequently, the Region does not have documentation of its oversight of NMED's management of the MWL monitoring wells. For example, EPA conveyed its Oversight Review concerns regarding the MWL monitoring wells to NMED orally, and NMED was not required to formally respond to the technical team's concerns regarding the MWL monitoring wells. Consequently, any resolution of the concerns is undocumented.

Misleading Communications. Region 6's communications with CANM did not adequately convey relevant and available information regarding CANM's stated concerns. Early drafts of a letter from Region 6 to CANM initially indicated that the Oversight Review would be provided to CANM. However, when a letter was sent from Region 6 to CANM, the document was not included, and the letter itself gave limited information regarding Region 6 findings and recommendations. The Chief of the Federal Facilities Section informed the OIG that she chose to simplify the Region's response to CANM because including overly technical information when corresponding with the public sometimes creates confusion. In an e-mail to the OIG, the Region explained, "We did not include a big 'report' analyzing all the things [CANM representative] says NMED is doing wrong, as he had requested. [CANM representative] has already indicated he will be FOIAing all of our drafts, notes, etc. regarding the report, so we will see where that all turns out."

EPA's Public Involvement Policy instructs EPA managers and staff to "work to ensure that decision-making processes are open and accessible to all interested groups." This policy also instructs EPA to approach all decision making with a bias in favor of significant and meaningful public involvement. The Region's actions do not do that.

The Region's response was misleading as it did not inform CANM that it found some of CANM's concerns valid. The Chief of the Federal Facilities Section stated her response was not intended to mislead CANM.

Inappropriate Classification. The Project Engineer withheld the Oversight Review from the public by marking it Confidential, a security classification category. Regional counsel stated to the OIG that the marking was intended to show that the document was a deliberated draft. Classified information is not releasable to the public. On April 27, 2009, the regional counsel confirmed that the document contained no classified information. As such, the Regional Administrator should have the national security marking removed from this document.

Region 6 Accepted NMED's Recommendations and Dismissed Its Own Concerns without Supporting Documentation

In 2007, the Region's technical review team found several areas of disagreement with NMED decisions regarding the monitoring wells at the MWL. Despite disagreement between the Region and NMED on several recommendations, the EPA Region 6 Director of the Multimedia Planning and Permitting Division found that NMED's overall action and decisions for administration of the authorized program were technically sound. However, the Region did not record evidence to support this finding.

The Region accepted NMED's recommendations and dismissed its own concerns regarding NMED's management of the MWL monitoring wells. The Region claimed to have no documentation to support these actions and provided none to the OIG. The Chief of the Federal Facilities Section stated that her organization must use experience and judgment in making oversight decisions. The Chief of the Federal Facilities Section also stated the Region adopted NMED's position on the MWL monitoring wells as long as NMED meets "applicable technical and administrative requirements." The OIG does not take issue over the use of experience and judgment in oversight roles or the acceptance of NMED's positions, assuming those issues are within the limits of NMED's discretion under the delegation of authority. However, the Project Engineer for Sandia intentionally did not document concerns with NMED's management of the MWL monitoring wells specifically to withhold the information from the public. Therefore, the Chief of Federal Facilities Branch has no documentation to support the Region's acceptance of the NMED's recommendations.

The Chief of the Federal Facilities Branch's failure to document concerns with NMED's management of the MWL monitoring wells or the basis for the concerns resolution is an internal control deficiency that deprives management and the public of the ability to make informed decisions. The Project Engineer for Sandia and the Chief of the Federal Facilities Branch provided no documentation to support its judgment to accept NMED's position despite its concerns. In five cases, EPA rescinded its recommendations with regard to the MWL monitoring wells in favor of NMED's proposed plan. Although the Region told us the issues were resolved orally (meetings, conference calls, and individual phone calls), the Region was unable to provide any documentation to support or document the rationale for these compromises. We found that one Oversight Review team member felt the team was pushed to agree with NMED's position regarding the MWL monitoring wells.

The Chief of the Federal Facilities Section informed the OIG that most of the concerns detailed in the Oversight Review have been addressed by actions taken. One e-mail from the Project Engineer for Sandia to the OIG noted, "Yes, we have some differences of opinion, but NMED has delegated authority and the latitude to do what they deem is appropriate (as long as it protects the environment and meets our rules, of course)."

Deferring to NMED based on its delegated authority would be acceptable if EPA had the documentation to support the determination that NMED had acted within the scope of its authority. However, as stated previously, some Region staff members did not document concerns with NMED's management of the MWL monitoring wells or the basis for the resolution of these concerns.

Recommendations

We recommend that the Regional Administrator, Region 6:

1. Comply with EPA's national security, public involvement, and records management policies, including removing the national security marking from the December 2007 Oversight Review.
   a. Ensure that the opinions of technical and nontechnical staff are documented to support EPA's oversight decisions.
   b. Develop or update oversight standard operating procedures to ensure compliance with these policies.

2. Evaluate the extent to which the Region has not recorded oversight information, or misclassified information, to determine the scope of administrative action or training necessary to remedy the situation.

Agency Comments and OIG Evaluation

The OIG made changes to the report based on the Agency's comments where appropriate. Appendix A provides the full text of the Agency comments and the OIG response to those comments.

EPA does not agree with the recommendations in this report. The Region 6 Regional Administrator has requested that the matter be elevated in accordance with EPA's Audit Management Process. Region 6 believes it maintained information sufficient to respond to CANM's inquiry about the wells. The Region believes it complied with public involvement and records management policies to the extent they apply.

The report concluded that Region 6 oversight was not sufficiently documented because it did not show how the Agency concerns regarding the mixed waste landfill were resolved. The report states, "Specifically, the Region did not provide the OIG with documentation to support the Region 6 response to CANM that the Region found NMED's overall actions and decisions to be technically sound and consistent with requirements." EPA policy is that agency records must contain documentation that is "adequate and proper." That is, the documentation must show a clear picture of how the Agency conducts its business and makes its decisions.

The Region 6 response is that it prefers to initially discuss these matters informally to gather information without unnecessary confrontation. The Region believes that its informal approach provides clarification and resolves concerns. The Region says that the informality is not an attempt to defer to the State without documentation; rather, that is the nature of its "oversight." Region 6 did not explain why it believes its actions and information collected should not be documented as required by EPA policy. OIG cannot assess the adequacy of oversight based on undocumented informal conversations and information. In our opinion, oversight and transparency require documentation that shows a clear picture of how the Agency conducts its business and makes its decisions. The existing documentation does not show how Region 6 resolved its specific concerns to reach a conclusion that the overall actions and decisions for administration of the authorized program were technically sound and consistent with applicable RCRA requirements.

Region 6 denied its staff took inappropriate steps to withhold information from the public. The report addressed the Region staff's failure to document the discussions and resolutions with NMED of EPA's concerns. Region 6 comments focused on a single document (the oversight review inappropriately marked "confidential"). Those comments did not address evidence presented in the report that Region 6 staff intentionally stopped documenting discussions to avoid responding to the public's FOIA requests. It does not matter if a government agency collects information informally or otherwise; an agency is required to maintain documentation to clearly show how it does business.

Region 6 also stated that it was puzzled about the documentation issue, because it had no final action or permitting decision to make with regard to the wells. The region's role, according to Region 6, was to provide oversight of the State's implementation of the program and make appropriate responses to inquires from the public concerning the State's implementation. Later

Region 6 states that the Oversight Review was not released to the public because it was one of many draft versions, withheld under Exemption 5 of FOIA, 5 U.S.C. § 552(b)(5). Apparently the resolution of concerns with NMED did not involve decisions requiring documentation of Region 6's actions, but did involve decisions that allowed the Region to exempt some documents from public disclosure.

Access to information is crucial for informed public involvement. EPA's policies say public involvement begins when individuals and organizations seek information from EPA about a topic or issue, or when they receive information from EPA because the Agency identifies them as a potentially affected party. EPA's outreach activities are supposed to serve and engage these individuals and organizations. As individuals and groups become more involved, they seek more detailed information, increased access to decision makers, and more influence on the ultimate decisions. The failure to maintain adequate and proper records also negatively impacts on public involvement.

Lastly, with regard to compliance with other EPA policies, Region 6's admission that it commonly marks non-classified information confidential puts it in violation of EPA security policies. The EPA National Security Handbook, February 1, 2005, sets forth the procedures for the proper handling of national security information. Paragraph 4-500 – 3 (Marking Prohibitions) specifically states, "The terms "Top Secret," "Secret," and "Confidential" should not be used to identify non-classified information." Using unique markings for classified information allows personnel to recognize it and ensure it is properly safeguarded.

In summary, the Region 6 Administrator's comments substantiate the necessity for both Recommendations 1 and 2. The Region's rationale for mismarking information is that other people do it. The Region's rationale for the lack of documentation is that regional oversight is informal and not confrontational, so it does not need to be documented. As a result transparency and public involvement are adversely affected.

Status of Recommendations and Potential Monetary Benefits

		RECOMMENDATIONS				POTENTIAL MONETARY BENEFITS (in $000s)	
Rec. No.	Page No.	Subject	Status[1]	Action Official	Planned Completion Date	Claimed Amount	Agreed To Amount
1	5	Comply with EPA's national security, public involvement, and records management policies, including removing the national security marking from the December 2007 Oversight Review	U	Regional Administrator, Region 6			
		a. Ensure that the opinions of technical and nontechnical staff are documented to support EPA's oversight decisions.					
		b. Develop or update oversight standard operating procedures to ensure compliance with these policies.					
2	5	Evaluate the extent to which the Region has not recorded oversight information, or misclassified information, to determine the scope of administrative action or training necessary to remedy the situation.	U	Regional Administrator, Region 6			

[1] O = recommendation is open with agreed-to corrective actions pending
C = recommendation is closed with all agreed-to actions completed
U = recommendation is undecided with resolution efforts in progress

Agency Response to Draft Report

March 3, 2010

<u>**MEMORANDUM**</u>

SUBJECT: Draft Hotline Report Project No. FY08-00025
                             Sandia   ixed Waste   andfill

FROM: Al Armendariz /s/
                             Regional Administrator
                             Region 6

TO: Bill A. Roderick
                             Acting Inspector General
                             Office of Inspector General

        This memo is in response to the OIG's Draft Hotline Report entitled '*Region 6 Needs to Improve Management of Oversight at Sandia Landfill*' dated January 28, 2010. The draft OIG report charges that a Region 6 manager and project officer 'took inappropriate steps to keep details' of a draft technical evaluation from the public and violated EPA's national security, public involvement, and records management policies, including inappropriate use of national security markings. As explained in more detail in the attached summary, these charges are simply not true. Documents were not misclassified and details of EPA's evaluation were not withheld from the public. The draft, pre-decisional, technical review that the OIG auditors referenced was subject to review in the Regional Office and EPA headquarters under the Freedom of Information Act and was exempt from release under FOIA because it does not reflect the Agency's final position. Region 6 is therefore unable to concur on the recommendations included in this draft report and respectfully requests that the matter be elevated in accordance with EPA's Audit Management Process.

        Should you have any questions regarding the attached response please contact Carl Edlund, Director of the Multimedia Planning and Permitting Division, at 214-665-7200, or Susan Spalding, Associate Director for RCRA, at 214-665-8022.

Attachments (see next page)

cc: See next page

Page 2
Memo to ill oBeriBk
Draft OIG Report Sandia

Attachments

1. Region 6 Comments on Draft Report
2. EPA Region 6 RCRA State Hazardous Waste Program Oversight Process
3. EPA Region 6 letter to CANM dated December 13, 2007
4. EPA Region 6 letter to CANM dated February 8, 2008
5. FOIA Appeal Determination dated August 7, 2008
6. FOIA Appeal Determination dated November 12, 2009
7. OIG Hotline Closeout Letter dated June 20, 2007

cc: Wade Najjum, OIG
     Eric Lewis, OIG
     Pat Hirsch, OGC
     Kevin Miller, OGC
     Cynthia Anderson, OGC
     Bob Frederick, OGC
     Matt Hale, ORCR
     Jim Berlow, ORCR

Corrected Attachment with Comments from OGC, [name of OGC personnel redacted here]

Attachment 1 – Region 6 Comments on Draft OIG Hotline Report – Sandia MWL

<u>**General Comments**</u>

1. A key concern in the draft Hotline Report (HR) is the national security marking on a document referred to as the Oversight Review. The word "confidential" was used on the document to indicate that the document was draft and pre-decisional.

> **OIG Response. It is a fact that the document was inappropriately labeled "confidential." Confidential is a national security marking. The EPA National Security Handbook states that, "The terms "Top Secret," "Secret," and "Confidential" should not be used to identify non-classified information." It appears Region 6 leadership is unfamiliar with EPA's National Security Information Handbook.**

As indicated in the HR, only the Administrator of EPA has the authority to classify information as "confidential" for national security purposes. There was no intention or authority on the part of Region 6 staff to classify the Oversight Review as confidential national security information. The term "confidential" is commonly used throughout the Agency for many documents, such as personnel-related documents and other internal correspondence. Further, markings on a document, such as "confidential" or "deliberative" have no impact on whether or not the document is released to the public.

> **OIG Response. OIG cannot verify the intent of Region 6 staff in marking the document "confidential." A Region 6 staff member provided OIG with an email that the document was marked "confidential" to remind the writer and others not to file it with other RCRA paperwork since "it was a draft with some unanswered questions." There was nothing in the document to justify marking the document "confidential" under agency information security policy. Other agency personnel handling the document would have to assume that the document was classified. Further, no document with a classified marking can or should be turned over to the public until the document is declassified and the marking is removed.**

The Region 6 RCRA Program and Office of Regional Counsel worked closely with EPA's Assistant General Counsel for Information Law to comply with EPA's FOIA procedures and public involvement policies as they related to release of Sandia documents. Because of this coordination with EPA Headquarters, a copy of this response is provided to the OGC to ensure that any issues regarding the FOIA and public involvement processes are effectively communicated and resolved at the appropriate level within the Agency. OGC has also expressed an interest in your concerns related to the use of the term "confidential" on internal deliberative documents.

OIG Response. The findings in the report are based upon the actions of Region 6 personnel. Prior FOIA releases are not addressed in this report nor has OGC contacted OIG on this subject or national security classification markings.

2. The HR alleges that Region 6 oversight was not sufficient to determine whether Citizen Action New Mexico's (CANM) allegations had merit or whether the New Mexico Environment Department's (NMED) actions and decisions were technically sound. Region 6 oversight of the Sandia Mixed Waste Landfill (MWL) was extensive, particularly for an authorized program, and was documented in the EPA Region 6 RCRA State Hazardous Waste Program Oversight Process. In addition, several supporting documents including the response letters to CANM dated December 13, 2007, and February 8, 2008, demonstrate the degree to which Region 6 documented its oversight and communication with CANM. It is not clear what additional documentation the OIG believes Region 6 should have created to document oversight of the Sandia MWL. Documents referenced above are provided as attachments 2, 3 and 4.

OIG Response. Region 6 misstates the report. The issue in the report is documentation of the Region's oversight. Specifically that documentation was insufficient. Since the agency did not document how it resolved its concerns. OIG cannot determine if the Region's actions were adequate. The Region does not address the specific documentation issues in the report. The Region 6 Project Engineer stated that documentation of discussions with NMED concerning the monitoring wells at the MWL were no longer kept in an effort to prevent CANM from issuing FOIA requests. The Chief of the Federal Facilities Section added that NMED was reluctant to engage in open discussions with EPA because of frequent CANM FOIA requests. In contrast to the Region's actions, the EPA records management policy states at a minimum the Agency must, "Create, receive, and maintain official records providing adequate and proper documentation and evidence of EPA's activities."

3. As discussed on the February 17, 2010, call between Region 6 and the OIG, the Oversight Review document was subject to two FOIA appeals determinations made by EPA Assistant General Counsel for Informational Law. This appeals process and the resulting decisions are an important point that should be included in the draft Report. Copies of the appeal determinations are provided as attachments 5 and 6.

OIG Response. The OIG did not make any recommendations regarding the release of the Oversight Review.

4. The OIG Hotline closeout letter for the Sandia MWL dated June 20, 2007, (provided as attachment 7), refuses to examine CANM's complaint dated June 2006 because it was superseded by a pending lawsuit; two other ongoing investigations; and a notice of intent to sue EPA, NMED, and others; all filed by CANM concerning the same allegations. Those matters were pending in May 2007, when CANM's second OIG hotline complaint initiated this HR. However, the HR does not include any information regarding the outcomes of those matters, nor does it discuss their impact, if any, on OIG's investigation for the HR. We believe that the hotline complaint CANM filed in June 2006 was substantively similar to CANM's complaint filed in May 2007, which initiated the HR. Therefore, we believe the status and outcome of the

matters referenced above is relevant and should be discussed in the HR.

OIG Response. This report addresses internal regional practices that violated EPA policies and guidance for marking national security information, public involvement and records management. The outcome or status of other allegations are not material to these issues.

Sandia MWL Factual Background and Draft OIG Report Errors

The HR is erroneous and misleading because it does not provide any context for Regional oversight activities. It focuses on the Sandia MWL groundwater monitoring wells and, specifically, Region 6's 2007 review of the wells in response to complaints from CANM but fails to provide any technical details. Based on this single narrow aspect, the MWL monitoring wells, the report mistakenly concludes there are flaws in our overall oversight program relating to national security, public involvement, and record keeping.

OIG Response. That is incorrect. OIG did not conclude there were flaws in the oversight program. The purpose of the review was the Region's oversight of the MWL monitoring wells. OIG concluded that there was not sufficient documentation for OIG to make a determination regarding the Region's oversight. However, the Regional Administrator comments that not documenting "informal" communications is how Region 6 oversight is practiced and mislabeling of documents is an acceptable practice if it is widely done is an indication of poor oversight practices. OIG believes that if these practices were widespread they would constitute a serious material internal control weakness. Consequently, we recommended that the Regional Administrator, "Evaluate the extent to which the Region has kept information from the public, not recorded oversight information, or mislabeled information as classified, to determine the extent of administrative action or training necessary to remedy the situation." The Regional Administrator denied there was a need to do that.

The MWL is a 2.6 acre solid waste management unit (SWMU) located on the 8600 acre Sandia National Laboratories, New Mexico facility. Region 6's oversight of the New Mexico program involves a great deal more that just the Sandia facility, this small closed landfill, and its individual monitoring wells. Extensive information regarding the details of our oversight activity as well as specific actions related to the 2007 monitoring well review were previously provided to the OIG, verbally and in writing.

OIG Response. The specific allegations pertain to the Region's oversight of NMED's management of the MWL monitoring wells. As noted above we found insufficient documentation and noncompliance with EPA policies which we consider to be a material internal control weakness. If the weakness proves to be pervasive throughout the Region, then the effectiveness of all programs managed by the Region could be questioned. To that end, we recommended that the Regional Administrator determine whether those practices were widespread; however, he declined.

National Security Claim

The HR alleges that Region 6 violated national security policies and intentionally withheld information from the public by marking one document "confidential." Because the document was a draft, and still pre-decisional, that allegation is overreaching and distorts the facts.

OIG Response. The Region avoids addressing the fact that Region 6 staff intentionally did not document discussions with NMED to avoid releasing them to the public under FOIA. Region 6 also mislabeled a document as "confidential" and, the national security marking should be removed. OIG does not know what the intent was, but Regional personnel equated the term confidential to deliberative draft and said the purpose of the marking was to keep the document from CANM. Regional personnel provided OIG with emails indicating that the document was originally prepared for release but later decided to withhold the document. Regional personnel stated that they did not present the document to CANM because they did not want to burden the public with overly technical information. Regional personnel added that the document was a deliberative draft.

The December 12, 2007, document marked "confidential" and described as the "oversight review" in the HR was the last draft summary of Region 6's staff review of the old groundwater monitoring system at the MWL. This particular document was marked "confidential" and "draft" because it was an internal deliberative working draft, not because the authors intended to make a national security classification. Several members of our staff with geology, engineering, and groundwater monitoring experience reviewed available information for the MWL and provided their opinions and perspective, which were documented in various draft summary documents. In fact, the draft document has never been finalized. Accordingly, as the IG investigators are well aware, this document went through the Regional FOIA review process and was withheld as deliberative under Exemption 5 of FOIA, 5 U.S.C. § 552(b)(5) by the Deputy Regional Administrator, Management Division. After the Freedom of Information Act (FOIA) requestor filed two administrative FOIA appeals, EPA's Office of General Counsel upheld the Region's application of Exemption 5 and denied both appeals. These facts do not appear in the HR, thus making the report misleading by omission. Moreover, a marking on the document does not control whether the document will be released under the FOIA. As happened here, the Region (or appropriate program office) will still review the record to determine whether it is exempt or releasable notwithstanding a designation.

OIG Response. We have previously addressed the markings on the document. We made no recommendation to release the oversight review to the public.

Public Involvement

Since New Mexico's RCRA authorization, NMED has been the permitting authority for this site and Region 6's role is oversight of the entire authorized RCRA program for New Mexico. The NMED regulatory permitting process includes appropriate public notice and comment opportunity. Historically, opportunities for public participation have been plentiful. The Final Order issued by the NMED Secretary of the Environment in 2005 for MWL remedy selection provides for additional, greater opportunity for public participation than required by the regulations. The Department of Energy (DOE) commissioned a Citizen's Advisory Board (CAB), which met at least quarterly from the late 1990s until September 2000 to discuss issues at the MWL. This forum allowed the public, regulators, and local experts to openly discuss and debate technical issues and solutions for the MWL. EPA was an ex officio member and CANM, as a full CAB member, was an active participant in these discussions. The DOE has continued to

hold quarterly and semi-annual public meetings to discuss environmental issues at Sandia. At the MWL, Region 6 has participated in site activities far beyond that which is normally done in overseeing an authorized State's implementation of the RCRA program.

OIG Response. The above comments are not relevant to Region 6 internal management control weaknesses.

Region 6 has been actively involved with the MWL site for many years; therefore, the HR statement that the Region only became involved with the MWL after we received a request from Senator Bingaman is incorrect. CANM asked Region 6 to assess the monitoring wells in March 2007 and apparently contacted the Senator at nearly the same time, preempting our response to CANM. Further, Region 6 had already been in contact with CANM and provided them with more than 500 pages of documents under FOIA in February 2007. The extent of our prior involvement at the MWL is not reflected in the HR, probably because the OIG investigators only requested Region 6 records dating back to March 2007 (10/02/2008 email, names of OIG and Region personnel redacted here).

OIG Response. The report attributes the statement to the Region's Project Engineer for Sandia. The extent of her statement was that the Region became involved with the MWL monitoring wells after a request from Senator Bingaman. Although that should be discernable from the text, we will add "monitoring wells' after the MWL statement.

As stated above, the so called "oversight review" document was not provided to CANM because it was one of many draft versions, withheld under Exemption 5 of FOIA, 5 U.S.C. § 552(b)(5). Our response regarding the well was provided to CANM in the December 13, 2007, letter, which informed CANM that NMED's overall actions and decisions for administration of the authorized program were consistent with applicable RCRA requirements. We found no evidence to indicate that the MWL posed an imminent or substantial danger to citizens or the groundwater supply. Because NMED had already directed the DOE and Sandia to install a vegetated cover and replace several wells, we believed these concerns were already being properly addressed by the State.

OIG Response. The conclusion provided to CANM was that overall actions and decisions for administration of the authorized program were consistent with applicable RCRA requirements. That conclusion left unanswered some specific concerns Region 6 expressed in the Oversight Review with NMED's management of the MWL monitoring wells. However, the Region has no documentation to show what steps taken, if any, to resolve their specific concerns or how the overall conclusion was reached in spite of their concerns.

While the Region believes it was important to respond to CANM's letter regarding the monitoring wells, it must be given proper significance as a State oversight matter and reflect to what extent this narrow issue should receive the Region's limited oversight resources. While the Public Involvement Policy encourages outreach and technical support to the public they also recognize that the Agency's limited resources should be spent on the highest priority issues.

OIG Response. Region resources had already been consumed to develop the Oversight Review. Despite its concerns expressed in the Oversight Review, Region 6 provided assurances to the public. The above comment implies that the concerns were left unresolved due to resource issues.

To further put this investigation and Regions 6's oversight activities into proper prospective, the HR focused on a single SWMU, the 2.6 acre MWL, which operated from 1959 to 1988. The MWL has a total of seven monitoring wells. There was no known release of contamination to the groundwater, the landfill contents were well-documented, the depth to the regional aquifer was nearly 500 feet, the distance to the nearest drinking water well was 4.6 miles, fate and transport modeling showed a low risk of contaminant release, there were no surface water features in the area, and there was little mechanism for contaminant transport due to the desert climate. Elevated levels of chromium and nickel, found in some older wells in the past few years, were investigated with down-hole video cameras but considered anomalous because the videos showed substantial corrosion of the well screens and there was no other known source for chromium or nickel in the landfill. This conclusion was supported by documentation of this problem at other sites and similar experience at Sandia where chromium and nickel exceedences stopped when wells with stainless steel screens were replaced with PVC. Conditions found at the MWL would normally dictate this SWMU be a low priority for oversight review, but nonetheless it has received direct review due to CANM's multiple requests. All of this information was available to the investigators but does not appear in the HR.

OIG Response. The above statement is not relevant to noncompliance with EPA record management and public involvement policies.

Records Management

The HR report raises concerns about our recordkeeping practices. The Region believes it maintained information sufficient to respond to CANM's inquiry about the wells. In 2007, when the Region was developing a reply to CANM concern regarding the monitoring wells, the project engineer retained all internal documents such as the staff notes and draft review summary documents generated throughout the time we were attempting to put together a response to CANM. These drafts were shared with supervisors and management, and many deliberative discussions occurred verbally and in writing. As the staff continued to research the issues, the drafts were updated and the format evolved. The decision to provide our conclusions to CANM in a letter was made by Region 6 management. The fact that the Region subsequently responded to CANM in a letter format does not alter the predecisional character of the draft documents or justify the HR claim that Region 6 intentionally misled or hid information from the public. Release of predecisional material would discourage open, frank discussions on matters of policy between subordinates and superiors prematurely disclose proposed policies before they are finally adopted, and cause public confusion by disclosing reasons and rationales that were not in fact ultimately the grounds for EPA's action. Our December 13, 2007, letter to CANM indicated that NMED acted reasonably within its discretion as the permitting authority for the MWL. Further, the issues CANM raised either were previously settled or would become moot upon the imminent installation of new monitoring wells and the vegetated cover. Therefore, we saw no public benefit to rehashing past issues when there was no apparent environmental threat or harm. Instead, we chose to focus on data from the new wells when it became available in order to resolve any ambiguities.

OIG Response. The report criteria is the EPA records management policy. The Region's assertion that it maintained sufficient records does not demonstrate compliance with this policy. Intentionally not recording information to avoid FOIA is not recognized as an agency records management tool.

The HR claims that Region 6 intentionally discontinued recordkeeping are without merit. The claim that we did not document our decisions on the monitoring wells is also puzzling because we had no final action or permitting decision to make with regard to the wells. That decision was the responsibility of NMED because NMED now has the responsibility to issue RCRA permits within New Mexico. The Region's role was to provide oversight of the State's implementation of the program and to make appropriate responses to inquiries from the public concerning the State's implementation. The need for Region 6 to conduct ongoing documentation of this specific MWL was negligible because the corrective action plan was already in place and being implemented. Our mid and end of year program oversight reviews have demonstrated and documented that NMED has met the Region's oversight expectations for Sandia and its other RCRA facilities. All of this information, along with the technical review drafts, notes, and other documents, was provided to the investigators.

OIG Response. The Region ignores that its staff told OIG that they did not document communications with NMED to deliberately keep CANM from information through the FOIA process. The Records Management Policy requires the Region to document its oversight activities regarding the MWL monitoring wells, which it did not do.

The Region attempts to work with its States in a collaborative manner to address issues that might arise at a particular facility. We prefer to initially discuss these matters informally to gather information without unnecessary confrontation, as we did with the MWL wells. Often, that provides clarification and resolves the concerns. This is not an attempt to defer to the State without documentation, as the HR alleges, but rather that's the nature of "oversight." The interactions between EPA and NMED occur as a back and forth dialogue because, when doing environmental or groundwater monitoring, differences of opinion sometimes arise on the "best way" to proceed. We must use experience and judgment in our dealings with authorized States, and the Region believes it's appropriate to defer to the authorized entity as long as they act reasonably within their discretion and follow the appropriate administrative requirements. Once again, this was explained to the investigators, but it does not appear in the HR. It is unclear how the HR can conclude that we failed to generate adequate documentation for the OIG to make a determination if CANM's claims had merit but the OIG was able to determine that we deferred to NMED on our disagreements. The OIG appears to misunderstand the difference between responding to a citizen inquiry and the oversight of a state's entire authorized RCRA program. The HR factually only discussed our response to CANM's inquiry about the wells, while its recommendation directs that we "develop or update our oversight," presumably for all the Regional state programs.

OIG Response. The Region ignores that its staff told OIG that they did not document communications with NMED to deliberately keep CANM from information through the FOIA process. Further, the Region did not have sufficient documentation to show that it determined deferring to NMED was an appropriate decision.

The fact that the HR focuses exclusively on our response to a citizen inquiry also does not correspond to what it stated in the Scope section of the HR on page 2. The HR states that "We [OIG] limited our review to EPA's oversight responsibilities as defined in applicable regulations and the memorandum of agreement (MOA) with the State;" however, there was no discussion in the HR concerning EPA's oversight responsibilities as defined in those applicable regulations and the MOA. In fact, the Region's mid year and end of the year oversight reviews are required by the MOA. This information concerning our oversight of the New Mexico program was shared with the investigators but was not discussed in the HR, and thus it is misleading by omission. We believe that this information was left out because it demonstrates that the Region does a very good job in overseeing the New Mexico program. Even the title of the HR demonstrates a lack of understanding of the nature of state oversight, i.e., "Region 6 needs to Improve Management of Oversight at Sandia Landfill." The State manages oversight of the Sandia Facility and, even more narrowly, this one particular Landfill. The Region oversees the State's program.

OIG Response. The Region is again incorrect. The purpose of the review as stated in the notification letter to Region 6 and the draft report was to ..."determine if EPA Region 6 carried out its oversight responsibilities regarding the Sandia National Laboratory's mixed waste landfill." The sentence from the Scope and Methodology section of the report is taken out of context. The full context says ..."We conducted audit work from December 2008 to September 2009 in accordance with generally accepted government auditing standards. Those standards require that based on our objectives, we plan and perform the audit to obtain sufficient and appropriate evidence to provide a reasonable basis for our findings and conclusions. We reviewed documents, regulations, the New Mexico/EPA memorandum of agreement governing NMED's Resource Conservation and Recovery Act (RCRA) program, and annual and semiannual reviews. We interviewed EPA Region 6 RCRA program managers and technical experts who work with New Mexico. We also interviewed members of CANM."

"We believe that the evidence obtained provides a reasonable basis for our findings and conclusions based on our audit objectives. EPA has granted the State of New Mexico primary responsibility for enforcing the RCRA program within its boundaries. We limited our review to EPA's oversight responsibilities as defined in applicable regulations and the memorandum of agreement with the State."

The HR states that we mislead CANM because one of our earlier, internal "draft letters" initially said we would send an Oversight Review report but then we did not include the Review in our final letter. How a draft letter we never sent to CANM could mislead them is not clear. Instead of finalizing this version of the draft review document, we chose to provide a response in a letter to CANM on December 13, 2007. We were not attempting to mislead CAMN but rather circumstances were such that the State had decided to order Sandia to put in new wells, which we believed made the report irrelevant and finalizing it a waste of resources.

OIG Response. The report says that we found the Region's actions to be misleading, but not because the oversight review was not sent. As we state in the report, the Region's actions were misleading when the EPA concerns were consistent with CAMN's but that information was not disclosed nor was the basis for any resolution of those concerns documented.

Current Conditions at Sandia MWL

Four groundwater monitoring wells at the MWL have been plugged and abandoned. One new background well and three new downgradient monitoring wells were installed in 2008. New monitoring results for constituents of concern show no indication of contamination to groundwater from the MWL. There is also no indication of chromium or nickel beyond background levels, which supports the previous conclusion that elevated levels of chromium and nickel were due to stainless steel well screen corrosion. This information was provided to the investigators in June 2009 but is not discussed in the HR. Since then, the vegetated cover was completed in September 2009 and monitoring results continue to be below actionable levels, as expected.

OIG Response. The above statement is not relevant to the report issues.

Response to Recommendations

1. Comply with EPA's national security, public involvement and records management policies, including removing the national security marking from the December 2007 Oversight Review.
    a. Ensure that the opinions of technical staff and nontechnical staff are documented to support EPA's oversight decisions.
    b. Develop or update oversight standard operating procedures to ensure compliance with these policies.

Region 6 Response: Region 6 feels that we did comply with public involvement and records management policies to the extent they apply. As stated above, the term "confidential" was used on the Oversight Review document to indicate that the document was draft and pre-decisional.

OIG Response. Region 6 comments are nonresponsive to the recommendations. EPA policies regarding records management, public involvement, and national security information apply to all EPA Headquarters Programs, Regions, Laboratories and other Offices. Region 6 failed to document its fact gathering and resolution of the differences

19

between its technical opinions and that of NMED. Region 6 staff intentionally did not produce documentation of their official activities so that could not be obtained through FOIA. Region 6 continues to defend marking unclassified documents "confidential" despite EPA policy that prohibits it.

Region 6 believes that the technical, nontechnical, and management oversight documentation for the Sandia MWL was sufficient to support EPA's oversight role, and we do not concur that additional measures are required. The Public Involvement Policy applies to EPA decisions. In this instance, our role was limited to oversight of NMED's authorized program; therefore, we did not have the authority to make a permitting decision. In a similar vein, the OIG's discussions about Regional actions (or inaction) "not to provide documentation" appear to be based on the OIG's belief that EPA – in its oversight role – had a duty to create more, unspecified original documents or records. The OIG does not cite any policy or guidance to support its conclusion that the Region did not meet the required threshold for creating documentation in the performance of overseeing a program authorized to the state. Given the very extensive oversight and resources the Region has provided related to this singular landfill, the OIG's hurdle seems excessively high and not sensitive to good stewardship of limited resources. The Region 6 State Hazardous Waste Program Oversight Process document completed at mid and end of year grant reviews as well as site specific documentation related to the Sandia MWL meet the requirements for this documentation (see attached EPA Region 6 RCRA State Hazardous Waste Program Oversight Process, Attachment 2).

OIG Response. Region 6 detailed comments stated that when issues arise the Region prefers to discuss them informally to gather information without unnecessary confrontation to provide clarification and resolve concerns. The Region states that is not an attempt to defer to the state without documentation, but rather that's the nature of "oversight." EPA Policy 2155.1 states that each office within EPA is required to establish and maintain a records management program with that will create, receive, and maintain official records providing adequate and proper documentation and evidence of EPA's activities. Region 6's preference to perform its official responsibilities informally does not relieve it of the requirement to document the activities it performs in accomplishing its duties. Proper documentation requires the creation and maintenance of records that document the persons, places, things, or matters dealt with by the agency; make possible a proper scrutiny by the Congress or other duly authorized agencies of the Government; and document the taking of necessary actions, including all substantive decisions and commitments reached orally (person-to-person, by telecommunications, or in conference) or electronically.

Because Region 6 complied with public involvement and records management policies, we do not concur with recommendation 1b. If the Agency determines that the use of the term "confidential" should no longer be used as a common practice, Region 6 will update standard operating procedures to make this decision clear to staff and management.

OIG Response. Agency policy is that "Confidential," "Secret," and "Top Secret" should only be used on classified documents. The violation of controls established to

safeguard classified information is not excused by past common practice and the comments document a Region-wide control failure. The Region's comments also indicate a serious deficiency in management control environment when management ignores agency controls in favor of ease of past common practice with the explanation that everyone does it.

2. Evaluate the extent to which the Region has not recorded oversight information, or misclassified information, to determine the extent of administrative action or training necessary to remedy the situation.

   Region 6 Response: The scope of this recommendation extends far beyond the Sandia MWL and the RCRA program. However, Region 6 did comply with public involvement and records management policies in the Sandia MWL case and believe our Regional public involvement and oversight processes are effective and in compliance with applicable laws, regulation, and policy. We do not believe a new evaluation is needed and do not concur.

   OIG Response. The report found that the Region had internal control deficiencies regarding public involvement, record keeping, and marking documents in the work performed. The Region's comments, particularly those regarding the widespread mislabeling of information as "confidential" and undocumented "informal" oversight demonstrate systemic material control weaknesses in these areas. The Region's comments, such as the refusal to address misuse of confidential markings with the explanation, in effect, that everyone does it, also indicates a deficient control environment.

   The control environment is the organizational structure and culture created by management and employees to sustain organizational support for effective internal control. The organizational culture is also crucial within this standard. The culture should be defined by management's leadership in setting values of integrity and ethical behavior but is also affected by the relationship between the organization and central oversight agencies and Congress. Management's philosophy and operational style will set the tone within the organization. Management's commitment to establishing and maintaining effective internal control should cascade down and permeate the organization's control environment which will aid in the successful implementation of internal control system.

Attachments to Agency Response to Draft Report

For this appendix, go to the following:

www.epa.gov/oig/reports/2010/20100414-10-P-0100_appB.pdf

Distribution

Office of the Administrator
Deputy Administrator
Regional Administrator, Region 6
Agency Follow-up Official (the CFO)
Agency Follow-up Coordinator
General Counsel
Associate Administrator for Congressional and Intergovernmental Relations
Associate Administrator for Public Affairs
Audit Follow-up Coordinator, Region 6
Acting Inspector General